MOUNTAIN MEN OF WYOMING

RICHARD FETTER

Johnson Books: Boulder

Cover photos: Clockwise from top left: Jim Bridger, Jim Beckwourth, Kit Carson, Thomas Fitzpatrick. (*Colorado Historical Society*)

Map: Llyn French

ISBN 0-933472-64-1

Printed in the United States of America by
Johnson Publishing Company
1880 South 57th Court
Boulder, Colorado 80301

To Mom,
and her own spirit of adventure.

CONTENTS

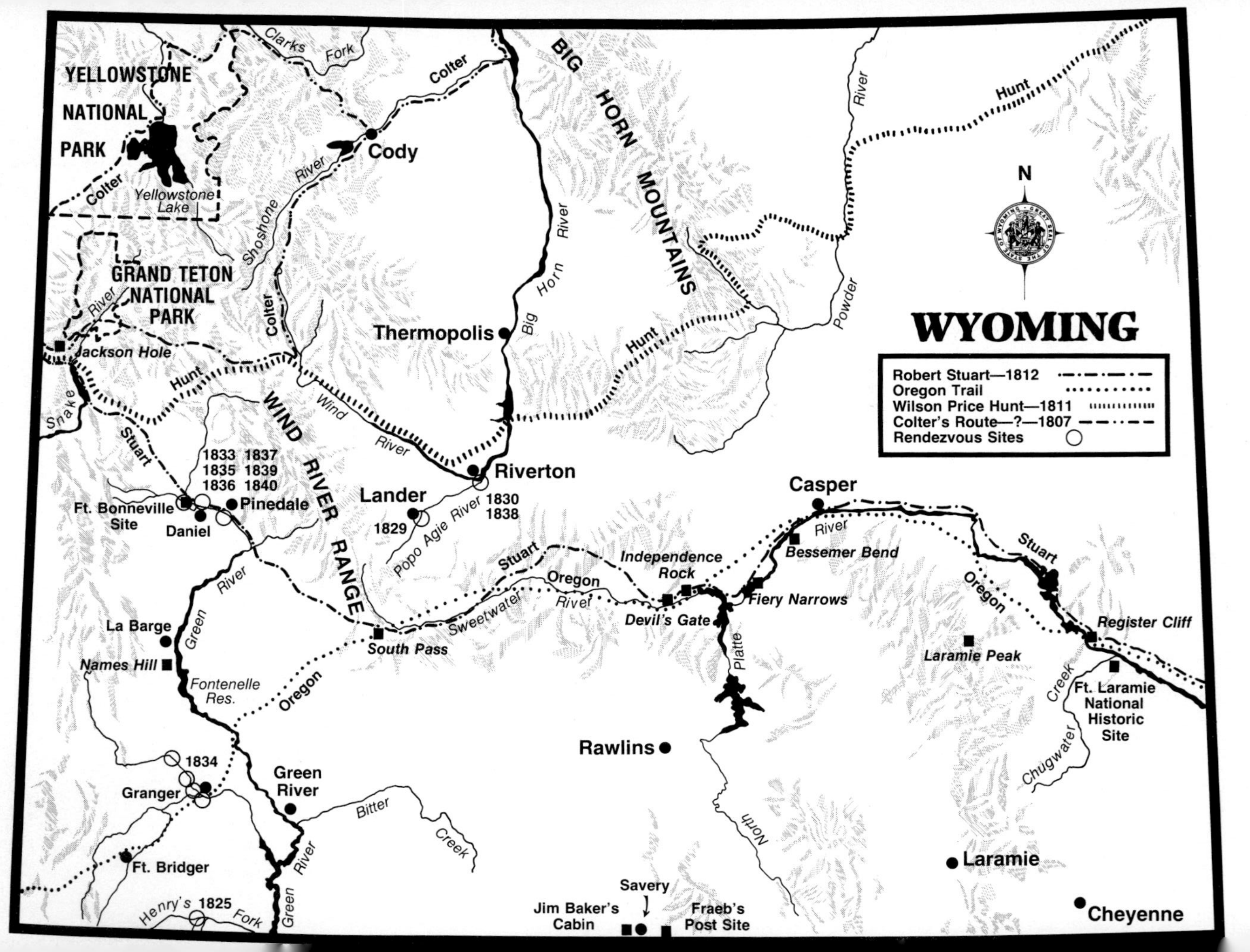
YELLOWSTONE NATIONAL PARK
Clarks Fork
Colter
Cody
BIG HORN MOUNTAINS
River
Hunt
N
GREAT SEAL OF THE STATE OF WYOMING
WYOMING
Robert Stuart—1812
Oregon Trail
Wilson Price Hunt—1811
Colter's Route—?—1807
Rendezvous Sites
Colter
Yellowstone Lake
Shoshone River
GRAND TETON NATIONAL PARK
River
Colter
Big Horn River
Thermopolis
Powder
Hunt
Jackson Hole
Snake
Hunt
Stuart
WIND RIVER RANGE
Wind River
Riverton
1833 1837
1835 1839
1836 1840
Lander
1829
Popo Agie River
1830
1838
Casper
River
Ft. Bonneville Site
Pinedale
Daniel
Stuart
Oregon
Independence Rock
Bessemer Bend
Stuart
Green River
Sweetwater River
Devil's Gate
Fiery Narrows
Oregon
La Barge
South Pass
Oregon
Platte
Register Cliff
Names Hill
Fontenelle Res.
Laramie Peak
Creek
Ft. Laramie National Historic Site
Chugwater
1834
Green River
Rawlins
Granger
Bitter
Creek
North
Ft. Bridger
Green River
Laramie
Henry's 1825 Fork
Savery
Jim Baker's Cabin
Fraeb's Post Site
Cheyenne

THE FIRST MOUNTAIN MEN

John Colter

In the spring of 1807, a solitary canoe came drifting down the Missouri River. It carried a white man who had spent the preceding winter trapping and exploring the rich fur country along the Yellowstone. For reasons unknown, the man had left his companions, Forrest Hancock and John Dixon, up in the mountains and was travelling alone.

The canoe continued downstream, borne by the gathering waters of the spring runoff. It passed the Mandan villages, where, less than a year before, its occupant had been returning with Lewis and Clark and had received permission from them to leave the expedition and trap the Yellowstone country with Hancock and Dixon. At that time John Colter had been one of the "stout, healthy, unmarried men, accustomed to the woods, and capable of bearing bodily fatigue in a pretty considerable degree" that Captain Lewis had required for his historic expedition. Now, further seasoned by a winter on the Yellowstone, Colter knew as much about the rivers, lakes, and mountains of the West as any white man of the time, and he was about to help turn a great page in Wyoming's history.

Wyoming in 1807 was part of the vast, largely unknown reaches of the Louisiana Territory, which President Jefferson had purchased from France in 1803. The land was a wild, forbidding place whose beautiful mountain ranges and broad prairies were inhabited by Indians and teemed with wildlife. Somewhere in the innermost regions of the land rose the continental divide. The Grand Tetons and Wind River Mountains, not yet so named, loomed in rugged beauty over their ancient valleys, and along the great natural landmarks that would be known as Devil's Gate and Independence Rock passed the less ancient trails made by animals and followed by the Indians. All was serene and untouched, unexplored, and unimagined, even by its new owners, who lived in a far more civilized world back east.

The land lay quietly waiting the time of the white explorers from that more settled world, and that time had come.

Colter, rounding a bend in the Missouri at the confluence with the Platte, was surprised to find a large expedition making its way up the river toward him. The expedition was even more surprised to come upon Colter, for a white man in a canoe was a rare sight on the Missouri in 1807.

The leader of the large group was Manuel Lisa, an experienced fur trader who would later prove to be one of the most significant men in the early years of the western trade. Lisa was familiar with the explorations of Lewis and Clark and was among the first to appreciate the significance of the rich fur trade possibilities they had discovered on their journey. Lisa was on his way up the Missouri to set up posts with tribes which had not yet had any contact with American traders. Would Colter join him as a guide? For Lisa, the chance meeting with someone returning from the unknown country where he was headed was a fine portent of things to come. Colter, who had been away from civilization for almost three years, must have been sorely tempted to continue down the Missouri. But something beckoned—adventure, fortune, or fate—and he turned west once again.

Colter led Lisa's party up the Yellowstone to the mouth of the Bighorn, where Lisa built Fort Raymond, also known as Fort Lisa, Fort Manuel, and Manuel's Fort. No trace of the fort remains today, and its precise location is not known, but this was the first American trading post on the upper rivers of the West and the first building in present-day Montana.

The fort was completed late in November 1807. Winter was coming and the men could do little trapping, so Lisa sent Colter out to invite the neighboring Indians in to trade. Colter took a thirty-pound pack, his gun, and some ammunition and trekked 500 miles to the Crow nation, then proceeded from them to several other tribes. The source of this data is Henry Brackenridge, whose arrival in the mountains would come quite soon. There is little doubt that Colter made such a trip; the great mystery concerns where exactly he went.

In 1814 William Clark published a "Map of the West" which shows "Colter's Route in 1807." Colter never saw the final map, for he was dead by 1814. Drawing upon this map and other sources, including diaries and journals of the time, most people agree that Colter went through Pryor Gap and passed the present site of Cody, Wyoming. Some believe he followed the South Fork of the Shoshone River, eventually arriving in Jackson Hole. He may have spent the winter on the Idaho side of the Tetons in Pierre's Hole. At the mountain man exhibit at the Grand Teton National Park Headquarters in Moose you will find a tantalizing piece of evidence that Colter almost certainly wintered in Pierre's Hole—the Colter Stone.

The stone was discovered on a farm near Leigh Creek, just inside the Idaho border, in 1931. It measures four by eight by thirteen inches, contains a human profile, and bears the name "John Colter" and the date "1808." As tempting as it may be to jump to conclusions, several authorities have discredited the stone. Aubrey L. Haines of the National Park Service has noted the other stones with dates found in the area, such as "Clark 1805,' "Henry 1810," and "Al the Cook but Nothing to Cook," and supports the theory that these were the results of "campside doodling" by the Hayden Survey in 1872. One of the most recent observers calls the stone an absolute hoax, the result of Aubrey Lyons's desire to obtain the horse concession at the Grand Teton National Monument in the early 1930s. Lyons allegedly carved the stone, planted it in a neighbor's field, and presented it to Sam Woodring after the neighbor happened to plough it up, not knowing who John Colter was. Woodring, the first superintendent of Grand Teton National Park, wanted a fur trade museum there and was delighted to receive such an artifact. Needless to say Lyons got the horse concession.

Whatever the truth may be, the stone is in the museum and Colter made his trip. Apparently he saw the boiling springs on the Shoshone River which came to be known as Colter's Hell. He brought back accounts of stinking waters, rivers of steam that shot straight into the air, and little ponds that gurgled and popped, earning for himself a reputation for being a great liar. Some time later, mountain man Jim Bridger also brought back fantastic descriptions of the Yellowstone country. As Bridger said to a friend late in life, "They said I was the damnedest liar ever lived. That's what a man gets for telling the truth!"

Colter, at least in this instance, was telling the truth. But more importantly, he had survived a Rocky Mountain winter alone, foreshadowing the era when men would go to the greatest extremes to survive the wilderness of the West. Manuel Lisa was highly impressed with Colter's stories of the richness of the land.

Encouraged by Colter's findings and what he had seen for himself, Lisa returned to St. Louis and with Andrew Henry and others formed a new St. Louis Missouri Fur Company in the winter of 1808-09. His company would become the most important one in the mountains in the early years of the trade.

Lisa set out for the Bighorn in 1809, determined to establish new posts on the Missouri and take the main part of his expedition to Fort Lisa. The following year the Blackfeet attacked, however, killing five men and causing the loss of much equipment. Fort Lisa had to be abandoned.

Ironically, the Indians probably attacked because of John Colter's epic journey. During his travels to the Indian nations, Colter had been among the Crows during an attack by the Blackfeet and had sided with his hosts. The Blackfeet were not about to forget this new white enemy, which was unfortunate, since Lisa had hoped to trade with all tribes. The hostility of the Blackfeet lasted throughout the history of the fur trade, and it eventually resulted in a harrowing incident which almost cost Colter his life.

He was trapping in the Blackfeet country with John Potts when five or six hundred Blackfeet appeared and told them to bring their canoe offshore. Seeing no chance for escape, the men complied. One Indian grabbed Potts's gun, Colter grabbed it back, and Potts, thinking they would be tortured to death, shot the Indian. Instantaneously, as Colter later reported, Potts was riddled with arrows.

Colter was seized and stripped. The Indians wanted to use him for target practice, but one chief grabbed him by the shoulder and asked if he could run very fast. Colter knew enough of the Blackfeet language and customs to know he was about to run for his life. Colter lied, saying he wasn't fast at all, so the chief gave him a lead of about 400 yards and then the Blackfeet came after him.

With the first whoop, Colter was off. Ahead of him lay five or six miles of plain, covered with grass, sagebrush, and prickly pear cactus, beyond which flowed the Jefferson Fork. The barefooted trapper ran for the river, his feet plunging into the sharp needles of the prickly pear, the Indians screaming in the distance behind him. Halfway across the plain, Colter dared to look back and found that he had been gaining distance on the Indians, except for one waving a spear a hundred yards behind. Colter pushed himself all the more, and his nose began to bleed.

With a mile still to go to the river, the footsteps were drawing nearer. Colter turned to see the Indian only 20 yards behind and closing in on him. Hoping to at least ward off the coming blow, Colter stopped in his tracks, wheeled around, and raised his arms. The Indian, surprised by the sudden move and startled by the sight of the bloodied Colter, stumbled and fell while trying to throw his spear. The point stuck in the ground and the shaft broke in the Indian's hand. Colter picked up the pointed end, thrust it into his attacker, and started running again. Just as he reached the river bank, the Blackfeet caught up with their fallen comrade. Colter plunged into the cold waters of the Jefferson Fork and swam downstream to an island. A raft of fallen drift timber had formed and lodged itself, and Colter managed to dive under the raft and find an air hole above the water among the tree trunks as the Indians arrived on the bank.

He spent the day there while the screaming Blackfeet searched the banks and even climbed about the raft, their feet visible to Colter through the chinks in the logs. Finally night came and the Indians left. Colter swam downstream, went ashore, and traveled all night. Without clothes or weapons, his feet full of thorns, Colter traveled for seven to eleven days, subsisting on roots and the inner bark of trees, until he reached Lisa's Fort on the Bighorn, 250 miles away.

After the Blackfeet attack on Lisa's party in 1810, Colter had at last had enough of Indians, mountains, and deprivation. He reportedly threw his hat on the ground, said he'd "be d----d if I ever come into [this country] again," and left for St. Louis, never to return to the mountains. He married a woman named Sally, farmed near his neighbor, Daniel Boone, had a son named Hiram, and died of jaundice in November 1813.

From all we know, John Colter was less than 40 years old when he died. Yet, in serving admirably with Lewis and Clark, guiding Lisa, and becoming the first known white man to discover the springs and geysers of Yellowstone, he enjoyed distinctions known to few men while ushering in one of the most adventurous and romantic periods in American history, the era of the mountain man.

The Astorians

In May of 1811, John Colter had a visitor in St. Louis. Wilson P. Hunt had been sent by John Jacob Astor, the wealthy New York fur baron, to follow the route of Lewis and Clark, build a trading post on the Columbia River, and set up a chain of trading posts that would link the Columbia River valley with the Missouri River, St. Louis, the Great Lakes, and New York.

We don't know what Colter told Hunt. Probably he warned him about the Blackfeet and told him to be prepared for more hardship than he thought possible. He could not have told him that history would repeat itself, or that Hunt's Astorians would wind up in Wyoming rather than follow the more northern route of Lewis and Clark, but in fact, that is what happened.

John Jacob Astor. (From Chittenden's *American Fur Trade*)

The year before, Andrew Henry, the partner of Colter's former employer, Manuel Lisa, had built a small post on the western side of the Tetons. Three of the trappers who had wintered there had returned across the mountains of Wyoming rather than follow the waters of the Yellowstone. Just as Colter had happened to meet Lisa in 1807, these three men—Hoback, Reznor, and Robinson—happened to meet Hunt's party and joined as guides.

They led Hunt along the route they knew, eventually retracing their steps across Wyoming. At the mouth of Hoback Canyon, south of Jackson, there is a roadside marker noting that the Astorians camped in this area on September 26, 1811. By then, the party had been traveling for five months. They had crossed the southern foothills of the Powder River Mountains, forded the Little Powder River, and ascended Clear Creek to near the present site of Buffalo. In September, guided by Edward Rose, they had crossed the Big Horns, then the Wind River Mountains to

Wilson P. Hunt. (From Chittenden's *American Fur Trade)*

the valley of the Green River, and traversed the mountains somewhere near Union Pass. From the summit they might have caught their first glimpse of the three peaks which later maps would call the Pilot Knobs, but which French trappers would call *les Trois Tetons*, the three breasts.

Hunt was openly afraid of Rose, a half-breed mixture of Cherokee, Negro, and white who had been a Mississippi River pirate before taking an Indian wife and living with the Crows. But without Rose and the Crows, Hunt's party probably would have perished somewhere in the Big Horns rather than reach the Hoback Canyon site and complete the first fully documented penetration of Wyoming. As it was, they barely made it from Wyoming to the mouth of the Columbia, arriving there the following February after extreme suffering, hardship, and the loss of several lives to the Snake River, hunger, and the elements.

The Hoback Canyon marker also notes that here, on October 12, 1812, Robert Stuart led a party of returning Astorians on their way back to St. Louis. In June Stuart had been given dispatches to deliver to Astor in New York. By October 12, he had led his men back along Hunt's route, following much of what would become the Oregon Trail. About 20 miles south of present Pinedale, Wyoming, Stuart met a band of impoverished but hospitable Snake Indians who were glad to trade some buffalo meat and leather for new moccasins in exchange for some trinkets.

More importantly, the Snakes told them of a large band of Crows to the east. Having already lost their horses to Crows, Stuart turned southeast to avoid a confrontation and found the broad, remote reaches and gentle inclines of South Pass. Suddenly, with surprising ease, they were following streams whose general direction was east rather than west.

There may always be some question among historians as

The returning Astorians. (*Fort Laramie National Historic Site, National Park Service*)

to whether Stuart and his men were actually the first to discover South Pass. Some feel Andrew Henry may have crossed it in 1811. Others believe it may not have been discovered until years later by Etienne Provost, Thomas Fitzpatrick, or Jedediah Smith. Whatever the cause may have been, and perhaps we shall never know, it is impossible to overestimate the importance of the discovery and the very existence of this pass. Thanks to this great natural corridor across the continental divide, thousands of wagons would later bring pioneers to Oregon, leading to the ultimate American domination of the Oregon Territory. Without South Pass and the thousands of settlers who passed so easily through it, much of today's states of Washington, Oregon, and Idaho might have remained under British control and become part of Canada rather than the United States.

On October 21, 1812, however, South Pass represented just a few more miles to Stuart and his men. Far more important to them was the fact that some of the men had shot buffalo in the past few days and not much snow had fallen in the night.

Ten days later Stuart came upon a striking fall of water which he called the "Fiery Narrows," indicated today by a state highway marker near Alcova, 30 miles east of Casper. Twenty miles farther on, at Bessemer Bend, Stuart's party built the first cabin in Wyoming in preparation for winter quarters. Later they relocated in western Nebraska because of unfriendly Indians. In April they reached St. Louis and learned that the United States had been at war with Great Britain for almost a year.

Jacques La Ramee

The fact that a powerful man like John Jacob Astor would send a party thousands of miles into a vast, unknown land in search of furs was an indication of the growing interest in the Rockies. The famous Hudson Bay Company was already entrenched in the Northwest, and Manuel Lisa and others had formed the Missouri Fur Company. But there was also a handful of individual trappers who sometimes banded together to try their luck.

According to C. G. Coutant's *History of Wyoming*, around 1815, one such man, a French Canadian, entered the United States with the North West Company, a major rival of the powerful Hudson Bay Company. In order to avoid conflicts developing between his company and the Hudson Bay Company, Jacques La Ramee supposedly organized a band of free trappers and went to the headwaters of the North Platte.

As a "free trapper" he was free to come and go and to barter and sell with whom he pleased, as opposed to an *engagé*, who owed allegiance to an employer. Living in this free, roaming manner, La Ramee traveled the North Platte and Laramie River country until the day of his untimely death.

In 1820 La Ramee told his companions that he was going up the Laramie River to trap beaver and would be back the following spring. When he failed to return, his friends went up the river to look for him and found him dead in a cabin about two or three days up from the river's mouth. According to Coutant, who wrote about the incident in 1899, Arapahoes were blamed for the death but denied it.

In 1868, Jim Bridger told John Hunton, the old-time resident of Fort Laramie, that, when in his teens, he was with the party that looked for La Ramee. According to Bridger, the party found an unfinished cottonwood log cabin and one broken beaver trap near it, but "no Laramie." Bridger said that two years later the Arapahoes told him some members of the tribe had killed the trapper and put his body under the ice in a beaver dam.

This is virtually all we know about the death of the man whose name, in its corrupted American version, is as prominent a place name today as there is in Wyoming.

We aren't even sure his first name was Jacques (Coutant used it, and it was the one popularly used) or where or when he was born. His last name has been variously spelled La

Ramee, La Ramie, and de la Rame. Yet this man about whom we know so little and perhaps never will know more, in five short years left his name to the Laramie River, Laramie Peak, Laramie Plains, Laramie County, Fort Laramie, the town of Fort Laramie, and the city of Laramie.

THE ENTERPRISING YOUNG MEN

Except for a few men like Jacques La Ramee, Wyoming and the entire Upper Missouri region saw hardly any white men for ten years following the War of 1812. Trade barriers between the United States and Canada arose and the market for beaver furs fell by 50 percent. Andrew Henry left Henry's Fork, and Manuel Lisa abandoned the Missouri Fur Company's post on the Yellowstone. Astor's attempt to establish a string of posts had failed, and west of the Rockies the British and Canadians were firmly in control of the territory.

But on February 13, 1822, the following advertisement appeared in the *Missouri Gazette & Public Advertiser*:

> To Enterprising Young Men
> The Subscriber wishes to engage ONE HUNDRED MEN, to ascend the river Missouri to its source, there to be employed for one, two, or three years—For particulars, enquire of Major Andrew Henry, near the Lead Mines, in the County of Washington, (who will ascend with, and command the party) or to the subscriber at St. Louis.

The notice was in the *St. Louis Enquirer* two weeks later and ran for six weeks in the St. Louis newspapers.

The advertisement was placed by William Ashley, a St. Louis businessman, and Andrew Henry, of Henry's Fort. Few advertisements have ever beckoned with so much adventure and romance, and response was prompt. In time it brought the individuals whose names would become legen-

TO
Enterprising Young Men.

THE subscriber wishes to engage ONE HUN-DRED MEN, to ascend the river Missouri to its source, there to be employed for one, two or three years.—For particulars, enquire of Major Andrew Henry, near the Lead Mines, in the County of Washington, (who will ascend with, and command the party) or to the subscriber at St. Louis.

Wm. H. Ashley.

February 13   ——98 tf

General William Ashley's famous advertisement in the *Missouri Gazette & Public Advertiser*, 1822.

dary among the mountain men: Jedediah Smith, David Jackson, William and Milton Sublette, Robert Campbell, Jim Bridger, Thomas Fitzpatrick, James Beckwourth, and others.

Many of the men came from Kentucky and Virginia, or from families that had migrated to the Missouri frontier, and they represented a broad range of educational and social backgrounds. Jedediah Smith, for example, was born in New York State of parents who were of old New England families. A deeply religious, serious individual, Smith contrasted greatly with someone like Beckwourth, the offspring of Sir Jennings Beckwourth and a slave mother, who became best known for his many adventures and very tall tales. Bridger, generally recognized as the greatest of all the mountain men, was illiterate, but James Clyman, whose extensive diary tells us so much of the times, was a surveyor under Alexander Hamilton's son. William Sublette, was a constable in St. Charles, Missouri; when he saw Ashley's ad, he quit his job and sold his bedstead for a dollar.

For some of these men, dreams of romantic experiences

Attack on the Ashley party. (*Fort Laramie National Historic Site, National Park Service*)

and high adventure were shattered before departure. One of Clyman's first duties was to search the riverfront bars of St. Louis to find boatmen to man the keelboats up the river. Riverfronts have always been rough areas, and the Missouri of 1822 was as bad as any. The crew finally assembled, according to several accounts, would have made Falstaff's band of roughnecks look like a bunch of polite schoolboys.

The times ahead were even worse. The first Ashley-Henry expedition lost a keelboat and $10,000 worth of property, and almost lost the crew, 20 miles below Fort Osage. Assiniboines tricked the party out of fifty horses, and the following spring Blackfeet killed four men and drove Henry away from the upper Missouri to the more southern Rockies of Wyoming's Snake River valley and Great Basin.

In the spring of 1823 Ashley advertised again and left St. Louis on another expedition with himself in command. In June the party was devastated by a cunningly planned Arikara attack. Well concealed in the timber, using their horses as a breastwork, the Arikaras unleashed such heavy fire that the boatmen couldn't move the keelboats ninety feet toward shore to rescue the men caught there. William Sublette was

The Summer Rendezvous. (From Victor's *River of the West*)

one of the lucky ones who managed to swim from a sandbar to the boats under a barrage of shot and arrows. In fifteen minutes the battle was over. Ashley had lost all of his horses and half the men who had been on shore.

Despite the prevalence of such inherent dangers, in three years Ashley was able to bring out 500 packs of beaver worth over a quarter of a million dollars. His fortune made, Ashley later sold out to Jedediah Smith, David Jackson, and William Sublette and returned to Missouri to pursue political ambitions. He was elected to Congress in 1831.

Rendezvous!

Perhaps Ashley's single greatest achievement to the mountain man era was his creation of the annual summer rendezvous, which was, without doubt, as colorful an annual event as has ever taken place. It has variously been described as a time of play, trade, and friendship, a drunken saturnalia, a time of extravagances, and a gathering of "a great majority of scoundrels." Undoubtedly, all are correct.

Indian Procession in honor of Captain William Drummond Stewart, 1837, by Alfred Jacob Miller. (*Colorado Historical Society*)

Ashley and Henry had gathered their own enterprising young men and sent them to the mountain streams because they had not wanted to rely on Indian trappers. Deciding also to avoid the expense and difficulty of building and maintaining forts or trading posts in the wilderness, they organized an annual rendezvous in the mountains at which Indians and trappers could meet and exchange their furs for goods brought in from St. Louis. The location varied according to where the greatest supply of furs could be found, but it was always in a well-known valley with abundant grass and game.

Except for two sites in northern Utah and Pierre's Hole on the Idaho side of the Tetons, all of the summer rendezvous sites were in Wyoming. The first was held in 1825 on Henry's Fork, near present day McKinnon in the southwestern corner of the state. Two were on the Popo Agie River near Lander. One was on Ham's Fork near Granger, and six were on the Green River, including the last two in 1839 and 1840.

If Daniel Potts's letters are to be believed, the rendezvous, at least in the early years, was not the drunken celebration it sometimes later came to be. In 1826 he wrote simply

Encampment at the foot of the Wind River Mountains. (*Colorado Historical Society*)

James P. Beckwourth. (*Colorado Historical Society*)

that "we celebrated the 4th of July by firing three rounds of small arms, and partook of a most excellent dinner, after which a number of political toasts were drunk."

As the years wore on, the rendezvous became far more boisterous. Captain Thing noted in 1834 that "two or three glasses of grog is the best introduction to trade," and the alcohol consumed was pure, powerful, and sometimes poisonous. Beckwourth said much of the time was spent in good natured competition involving running, jumping, racing, target shooting, and wrestling, but it was all too easy for things to get out of hand. At Pierre's Hole in 1832, for example, one of the men grabbed the kettle of alcohol, poured it over the head of a tall, lanky redhead, and started repeating the baptismal ceremony. All would have been fine except that another man touched the poor fellow with a lighted stick, setting him ablaze. Fortunately, enough sober men were around to beat him with pack saddles and put out the flames, saving him by the thinnest thread from a tragic baptism by fire.

According to Joe Meek, a mountain man, some of the more reckless men would spend $1,000 a day on their squaws, horses, alcohol, and themselves. With mountain prices as exorbitant as they were, it was easy to spend money. Sugar cost $1.50 a pound, tobacco was $3 a pound, and fish hooks went for $1.50 a dozen. But when you come upon coffee, sugar, and other staples for the first time in months, prices tend to be irrelevant.

Beaver skins provided the medium of exchange and were worth $4 to $6 in the mountains for a prime skin. Typically, a beaver was caught in a five-pound trap attached to a five-feet-long chain. The trap was placed in about three or four inches of water in a stream and the chain was fastened to a stick driven into the bed of the stream. The bait was a twig covered with castor or musk, which was very attractive to the beaver. To reach the twig, the beaver would spring the trap and eventually drown. The beaver would then be skinned and the skins bundled for transportation.

Joe Meek. (From Victor's
River of the West)

Beaver tail was a delicacy in the trapper's diet, which he savored along with deer, elk, antelope, and bear. Buffalo was the favorite, however, whether the hump, ribs, marrow, or steaks. Mountain men also drank the thick red blood, which tasted like warm milk. "French dumplings" were a specialty made of minced meat rolled on balls of dough and fried in buffalo marrow, and there were also *boudies*, the intestines of buffalo, cleaned, turned inside out, and stuffed with strips of well-salted and peppered tenderloin, then roasted and browned on a stick.

The more sensitive newcomer to the rendezvous might look at such men, their hands dripping with buffalo fat, their buckskin pants covered with grease and dirt, a bucket of grog nearby to wash everything down, and lament that the more refined aspects of living were far away. Party manners may have been a little rough, but the senses of these men were terribly acute. Washington Irving noted in *Astoria* how the returning Astorians thought they had come upon the Platte River because the water *tasted* like the Platte. A turned leaf, a pressed blade of grass, uneasy animals—all meant something, including, perhaps ultimately, the trapper's life.

In their own way, the mountain men were highly civilized. In a land without laws, courts, or judges, the code of the mountains called for fairness, generosity, and respect for property. A man was taken at his word and usually lived up to it. Contrary to popular image, the mountain men also read a lot. Osborne Russell, in his *Journal of a Trapper*, noted that winter reading included books by Byron, Shakespeare, and Scott, as well as the Bible and works on geology, chemistry, and philosophy.

The best tales were their own, however, and, living life on such an exaggerated scale, tall tales came quite naturally to the mountain men. Even today, when the rendezvous is recreated at various sites around the country, a liar's contest is always part of the festivities.

He may have been illiterate, but there was no greater storyteller than Jim Bridger. Bridger was fluent in Indian sign language, and Captain Howard Stansbury described an evening in 1853 when Bridger held a circle of Sioux and Cheyennes "for more than an hour, perfectly enchained, and evidently deeply interested in a conversation and narrative, the whole of which was carried on without the utterance of a single word. . . ."

Whatever he may have told to his fellow mountain men around the evening fires at the rendezvous, Bridger saved his best tales for the greenhorns and newcomers to the West. One British army captain asked him in 1866 to recount his most thrilling adventure. Bridger wove a tale of a day-long Indian fight and a night spent in great fear. At daybreak, as he and his companions led their weary horses out of a valley, the Indians came upon them and a two-hundred-feet waterfall blocked their exit. Bridger paused. The captain, beside himself with interest, cried. "Go on, Mr. Bridger; go on! How did you get out?"

"Oh bless your soul, Captain," Bridger replied, "we never did get out. The Indians killed us right there!"

Petrified forests with petrified birds singing petrified

James Bridger. (*Colorado Historical Society*)

songs, narrow escapes from Indians by running 95 miles "according to the closest calculation"—such were the lies that mountain men's stories were made of, to the delight of each other and the parties they guided over the plains years after the mountain man's day ended.

But the truth was that their own adventures were as extraordinary as the tales they loved to make up. For example, all of the mountain men were familiar with the incredible story of old Hugh Glass, a hunter with Andrew Henry in 1823. Sent out to hunt one fall morning, Glass surprised a mother grizzly that grabbed him by the throat, threw him to the ground, ripped off a mouthful of flesh, and tossed it to her cubs. When Glass tried to escape, she grabbed his shoulder and severely wounded his hand and arms. By the time Glass's companion and the rest of the party arrived and shot one cub and the mother, Glass was lying on the ground in great pain, unable to stand.

The party had to continue on, but Henry persuaded two men to remain with Glass until he died or could be moved. After two days Glass showed little improvement and the two men believed he would die. Taking his rifle and equipment, they left him and reported to the main party that Glass had died and they had buried him.

But Glass was alive. He dragged himself over to a nearby spring and lived for days on wild cherries and buffalo berries until he was strong enough to move. Then, driven by a desire to meet the two men who had left him to die, Glass began to drag himself toward Fort Kiowa, a post on the Missouri River 100 miles away. He had no provisions or weapon, and he was in the middle of hostile country. At one point he came upon a pack of wolves killing a buffalo calf and drove them off after they had eaten their fill. He "lived" in the carcass for the next few days, taking advantage of the fresh meat and shelter from the wind. Sustaining himself on this and the roots and berries he could find, Glass dragged himself along. Perhaps he made it to Fort Kiowa; at any rate, on October 15 he was with a party that had left Fort Kiowa October 10, bound by boat for the Yellowstone country.

Recuperating rapidly, Glass continued his vengeful journey after the two who had deserted him. Along the way he took an overland shortcut to Tilton's Fort, a trading establishment near the Mandan villages, and the following day his companions were attacked and killed by Arikaras. As Glass approached the fort, two Arikara squaws saw him and told the warriors. Glass was too weak to run, but just when the Indians were almost within gunshot range two Mandans seized him and brought him safely to the fort.

Glass left the fort that night and traveled for thirty-eight days until he reached Henry's new fort on the mouth of the Bighorn. There he caught up with his party, who were astonished to see him again. One of his two companions had gone on to Fort Atkinson, however, so on February 24, 1824, Glass accepted an offer to carry a dispatch to Fort Atkinson and left with four men. The party crossed Wyoming's Powder River valley and followed the sources of the Powder River to the Platte. Arikaras killed two of the men, one of whom was right next to Glass, who was hidden in some rocks. With nothing but knife and flint Glass headed northeast to Fort Kiowa, reached it in fifteen days, and arrived in Fort Atkinson in June.

Somewhere along the way Glass decided to concentrate his revenge on only the older of the two men, the other being quite young. But at the fort he found that his victim, John Fitzgerald, had enlisted in the army and was under protection of the law. The commanding officer gave Glass new equipment, and Glass decided to forget his revenge and entertain the troops with stories about his escape.

Glass's story is all the more extraordinary because it is true. The *Missouri Intelligencer* reported it on June 18, 1825, Colonel P. St. G. Cooke wrote about it in his *Scenes and Adventures in the United States Army*, and Potts referred to the event in his letters. Several observers at the time said the younger man was Jim Bridger, although this has never been proved.

The Arikaras finally caught up with Glass in the winter of 1832-33. Johnson Gardner, a well-known free trapper, related the circumstances to Maximilian, Prince of Wied, who wrote that Glass and two companions were hunting bears on the Yellowstone when they were shot, scalped, and plundered by a war party of thirty Arikaras concealed on the opposite bank.

Amazing as it was, Glass's long journey was not an isolated case. Osborne Russell, wounded in the thigh by a Blackfeet arrow, walked 200 miles from Yellowstone Lake to Fort Hall, crossing the Tetons and averaging 30 miles per day. James Clyman, separated from his companions by Indians in 1824, walked 700 miles alone through the wilderness to reach Fort Atkinson, living on parched corn and the carcasses of two badgers he clubbed to death with some old bones.

Being far from civilization and without medical supplies, an injured man could expect nothing but the most primitive attention to his wounds, with operations performed by companions who had never dreamed of being doctors. In the fall of 1823 Jedediah Smith and Thomas Fitzpatrick were left in charge of sixteen men detached to trap the Crow country. The men were proceeding single file down a brushy-bottomed valley late one afternoon when they came upon a large grizzly that attacked Smith, broke his ribs, and severely wounded his head, which was bleeding badly when Clyman reached him. As Clyman later wrote in his diary:

> I [found] the bear had taken nearly all of his head in his capcious mouth close to his left eye on one side and clos to his right ear on the other and laid the skull bare to near the crown of the head while leaving a white streak whare his teeth passed one of his ears was torn from his head out to the outer rim after stitching all the other wounds in the best way I was capabl and according to the captains directions the ear being the last I told him I could do nothing for his Eare O you must try to stitch up some way or other said he then I put my needle stitching it through and through and over and over laying the lacerated parts together as nice as I could with my hands water was found in about one mille

when we all moved down and encamped the captain being able to mount his horse and ride to campt whare we pitched a tent the onley one we had and made him as comfortable as circumstances would permit this gave us a lisson on the character of the grissly Baare which we did not forget. . . .

James Clyman. (From *Broken Hand* by Hafen and Ghent)

For the rest of his life Smith had an eye turned slightly upward and wore his hair long to cover his scars. Otherwise he recovered fully. Ten days after the attack he resumed command, and the following spring he was with Fitzpatrick when Ashley's men rediscovered South Pass for the first time since Stuart and the returning Astorians had passed through it in 1812.

For many people, Jedediah Smith was the greatest mountain man of all and certainly the greatest explorer. Andrew Henry left the mountains for the last time in 1824, and Ashley asked the young Smith to join him as his partner in 1825. The following year, Smith joined William Sublette and David Jackson in buying out Ashley's interest in the partnership, and Smith left Cache Valley, Utah, looking for beaver. He wound up in southern California, having pioneered a route across the desert. Then, with only two men, on foot, he returned across the Nevada desert to the Great Salt Lake. The men had gone without food and water, endured heat that they escaped by burying themselves in the sand, and arrived in Salt Lake City in an emaciated condition in June 1827 to meet friends who had given them up as lost. Smith, with his typical understatement, recorded in his diary that his return "caused quite a considerable bustle in camp" and that a small cannon was fired in salute. Ten days later Smith was off again, this time for California, Oregon, the Columbia River valley, and the Bitteroot Valley in Idaho. He did not return until the 1829 rendezvous in Pierre's Hole.

While Smith was off on his exploits, David Jackson stayed in the mountains to keep an eye on activities. Unlike the other enterprising young men, Jackson was in his late thirties, married, and had four children when he answered Ashley's call in 1822. Like Smith and Sublette, Jackson had been one of the lucky ones who survived the Arikara attack in 1823, breaking through the ranks of Indians with Sublette and swimming safely to the boats under a storm of balls and arrows.

Jackson had served Ashley as a field director, and his

experience, combined with his age, made him well suited for such a position with Smith and Sublette in their new Rocky Mountain Fur Company.

Little is known of Jackson's exact wanderings in the mountains, but we do know that the majority of his time was spent in and around the area we now know as Jackson Hole. A "hole" was a name for a mountain valley, and many came to be named for the trappers who lived in them. Of these, the most famous were Jackson Hole, Pierre's Hole, Brown's Hole (on the Green River), and Gardner's Hole (on a tributary of the Yellowstone near the entrance to Yellowstone National Park). There was also Jackson's Little Hole, located at the source of the Hoback River across the divide from Green River, which was the first camping place after leaving Green River for Jackson Hole or Pierre's Hole.

Fortunately, we can still appreciate the awesome beauty that must have attracted David Jackson to the area. The Grand Tetons rose majestically from their once glaciated valley to well over 13,000 feet, and the woods were filled with deer, elk, and a variety of small game. Most importantly, the streams were rich with beaver, and the area provided an excellent central vantage point for overseeing all operations of the company in the mountains.

Jackson Lake and the Tetons. (*Wyoming State Archives, Museums, and Historical Department*)

In the winter of 1830-31, Jedediah Smith prepared a map of the West showing the travels and discoveries of the Ashley men. In addition to his own extensive explorations, South Pass had been crossed several times. In 1824 Bridger had discovered the Great Salt Lake, thinking it was the Pacific Ocean until Clyman and Smith circumnavigated it. In 1825 Ashley himself made the first attempt by a white man to navigate the Green River. In 1827 Potts was with a party that went to the Yellowstone country. His letter to his brother, printed in the *Philadelphia Gazette* that year, is the first known written description of the region. Jackson, because of his own travels and explorations, was able to contribute much information on the Snake River area. The large lake in Jackson Hole was identified as Jackson Lake on Smith's map, and the name has been used since that time. Jackson Hole, Wyoming, of course, also takes its name from David Jackson, who is well remembered in one of the most beautiful places in Wyoming, the West, and, for that matter, the world.

With Jackson always in the mountains and Smith off exploring, Sublette became responsible for returning to St. Louis to bring out the goods for the annual rendezvous. A seasoned trapper, Sublette had not only narrowly escaped death at the hands of the Arikaras, but had almost died in a blizzard later the same winter. It was thus with considerable experience that he set out for St Louis in January 1830 and arrived on February 11, completing one of the first known crossings of the plains in mid-winter.

When Sublette returned to the mountains in July for the 1830 rendezvous in the Wind River valley, he startled the trappers by bringing ten wagons and two dearborns, all drawn by mules. The small cannon that had welcomed Smith in 1827 had been the first two-wheeled vehicle brought into the mountains. Sublette's expedition marked the first use of wagons over what would become the Oregon Trail. The loaded wagons weighed 1,800 pounds and had to be hoisted over embankments to reach their destination, but they arrived safely and the partners noted that the wagons could have crossed South Pass, had it been desirable for them to do so. In little more than a decade thousands of wagons would be doing just that, carrying emigrants to Oregon, paving the way for the American influence in the Northwest, and helping to end forever the mountain man's way of life.

Perhaps sensing the changing times, Smith, Jackson, and Sublette sold their company at the 1830 rendezvous to Thomas Fitzpatrick, Jim Bridger, Milton Sublette, Henry Fraeb, and Jean Baptiste Gervais, who formed the Rocky Mountain Fur Company. Later in the year Smith, Jackson, and Sublette arrived in St Louis with a profit of over $50,000.

The fact that at least some of the mountain men realized the significance of their explorations and discoveries is well illustrated by the letter Smith, Sublette, and Jackson wrote to the secretary of war that winter. They described their explorations, the country, routes to Oregon, and how best to deal with the British there. The letter was considered im-

Smith-Jackson-Sublette wagon train, 1830. (*Fort Laramie National Historic Site, National Park Service*)

portant enough to be printed as a Senate executive document and made available to Congress and the public.

The following year the three men left for the Santa Fe trade and Smith was killed at the Cimarron crossing by Comanches. Without Smith, Sublette and Jackson went their separate ways. The new Rocky Mountain Fur Company of Fitzpatrick, Bridger, and the others roamed the mountains for a few years but left little trace.

"DONE WITH THIS LIFE . . ."

We are done with this life in the mountains—done with wading in beaver dams, and freezing or starving alternately—done with Indian trading and Indian fighting. The fur trade is dead in the Rocky Mountains, and it is no place for us now, if ever it was. We are young yet, and have life before us. We cannot waste it here; we cannot or will not return to the States. Let us go down to the Wallamet and take farms . . . What do you say, Meek? Shall we turn American settlers?

This passage, allegedly by the old mountain man Robert Newell to Joe Meek, represents the culmination of the final decade of the mountain man era.

General Hiram Martin Chittenden, the eminent authority on the American fur trade, called 1832 the most eventful year in the history of the trade. For one thing, it marked the Battle of Pierre's Hole, the most noted battle between the Indians and trappers that ever occurred. The battle began when a party of Blackfeet appeared at the close of the rendezvous that July. Two of William Sublette's men, a Flathead Indian and an Iroquois half-breed named Antoine Godin, were sent out to meet a Blackfeet chief. Godin had an old score to settle with the Blackfeet, and as he reached to shake hands with the chief he told the Flathead to fire, killing the chief. Godin took the scarlet robe of his dead enemy as a trophy and an all-day battle broke out. Accord-

Thomas Fitzpatrick, trapper, mountain man, scout and guide. (*Colorado Historical Society*)

ing to several eyewitness accounts of the fight, at least ten Blackfeet were killed, a trapper named Sinclair lay dead, and William Sublette was wounded. Like the arrival of wagons at the Wind River rendezvous in 1830, the Battle of Pierre's Hole was a serious sign that the times were changing.

For one thing, the Rocky Mountain Fur Company was no longer alone in the Rockies. The American Fur Company of Astor was very much present, along with Nathaniel J. Wyeth and a group of New Englanders, plus Captain Bonneville, with a substantial backing from New York. In the old days there had been a keen rivalry with the Hudson Bay Company, but this at least had been marked by a certain sense of gentlemanly conduct. Now competition became vicious.

When the American Fur Company first came into the West, they had to learn where the best trapping places were. In the fall of 1831, Fitzpatrick and Fontenelle of the Rocky Mountain Fur Company became aware that Vanberburgh and Drips of the American Fur Company were trailing them. Fitzpatrick led his men out of the Powder River country and traveled 400 miles by forced marches to the Snake River. The following spring they came upon Vanderburgh and Drips searching for them once again. After the 1832 rendezvous, Fitzpatrick and Bridger were on the Jefferson Fork when they discovered Vanderburgh and Drips on their trail yet again.

Finally, the two mountain men had had enough. Striking into the very heart of the Blackfeet country, Fitzpatrick and Bridger led Vanderburgh and Drips from place to place until the Blackfeet attacked. Vanderburgh was killed and Bridger was wounded and carried an arrowhead in his back for nearly three years until Dr. Marcus Whitman removed it at the 1835 rendezvous on Green River.

The simple fact was that the mountains of Wyoming and the rest of the Rockies had opened up to an international fur trade and there weren't enough furs to go around. The Industrial Revolution had come to Europe and brought with it textiles at lower prices. Industry and technology thousands of miles away began to kill the market for the goods of the mountains.

But men kept coming to try their luck. A few miles west of Daniel, Wyoming, on State Road 354, a marker and monument point out the site of Fort Bonneville, named, like the Bonneville cabins outside Hudson, for the infamous Captain Bonneville. What exactly Bonneville was doing in Wyoming remains a mystery that may never be solved.

He arrived at Green River in July 1832 with leave from the army to explore the territory and learn about the Indians, trading possibilities, and other things of a general nature, at no cost to the army. Bonneville promptly built his trading post, Fort Bonneville, on the Green, but the location, while ideal for a rendezvous, was too high in altitude to live in comfortably in winter. The trappers called the place "Fort Nonsense" and "Bonneville's Folly." He subsequently sought a place on the Salmon River in Idaho.

Bonneville fared poorly as a trapper and achieved little with regard to his various official assignments, thus leading to speculation that he may have been sent out by the army as

Green River near Bonneville's fort. (*Richard L. Fetter*)

a spy to learn about British activities in Oregon. He was a capable, well-liked leader who is credited with being the first to bring wagons through South Pass to Green River. Probably his most significant action was to send Joseph Walker on an exploration, ostensibly to the Great Salt Lake, which wound up in California.

Walker's travels rivalled those of Jedediah Smith. Leaving Green River on July 24, 1833, with about forty of Bonneville's men, Walker led the way to the Great Salt Lake and crossed the desert to California, discovering the Yosemite region and the giant sequoias before carrying on to the Pacific Ocean. After spending part of the winter in California, Walker, guided by Indians, discovered Walker Pass, the northernmost free pass across the Sierra Nevada, on his return to Bonneville.

There is some doubt whether Bonneville intended that Walker should go to California, but he was certainly displeased that Walker returned with no furs. Largely unsuccessful in his own trapping ventures, Bonneville hardly had enough beaver skins to pay his men. He eventually returned to the states and the fact that he had overstayed his official leave of absence. In all likelihood, Bonneville's name would be far less known had Washington Irving not used it in the title of one of his books about the times.

From our distant perspective, the remaining years of the mountain men seem like a time when seeds were planted for future harvest. In 1832 William Sublette and Robert Campbell joined together to oppose the American Fur Company on the Missouri. Being experienced trappers, they fared far better than Captain Bonneville, and, more importantly, they built Fort William on the Laramie River. In 1833 this became Fort Laramie, an important military outpost until the end of the century.

The Rocky Mountain Fur Company, still owned by Fitzpatrick, Bridger, Milton Sublette, Fraeb, and Gervais, came to an official close at the Green River rendezvous in 1834. Fitzpatrick, Sublette, and Bridger bought Fort William from Campbell and William Sublette and joined the American Fur Company. Fraeb and Bridger eventually joined together again and in 1837-38 built Fraeb's Post on St. Vrain's Fork of Elkhead River, east of Savery on the Colorado-Wyoming border. Fraeb was killed there in 1841 in a battle against an overwhelming number of Cheyenne and Sioux.

John Jacob Astor, whose American Fur Company had finally acquired a significant position in the Rockies, retired from the trade in 1834. Advancing years may have influenced his decision, but Astor, ever perceptive, also noticed the ever-growing popularity of silk hats. "I very much fear beaver will not sell very soon unless very fine," he observed. "It apears that they make hats out of silk in place of beaver."

Times were also changing in the mountains. In 1835 the missionaries Dr. Marcus Whitman and Rev. Samuel Parker were at the rendezvous on Green River. The following year Whitman returned with his bride, Narcissa, and Rev. and Mrs. Henry H. Spaulding. The two women were the first two white women to travel the Oregon Trail. Mrs. Whitman's diary, filled with wonder at the Indians, the vastness of the country, and the exciting new way of life, was a forerunner of the impressions of thousands of travelers who

Christopher (Kit) Carson.
(*Colorado Historical
Society*)

were about to come. Fortunately, the 1837 rendezvous also saw the arrival of Alfred Jacob Miller, whose notes and paintings provide some of the most valuable glimpses of the times. Rendezvous scenes, camps, trapping beaver, threatened attacks, breaking up camp at sunrise—nothing escaped Miller's brushes in his hundreds of sketches and paintings.

But if the changing times brought the civilizing touches of women, missionaries, and painters, they also brought increasing numbers of desperadoes, horse thieves, bullies, and the famous encounter between Kit Carson and the French bully Shunar at the Green River rendezvous in 1835.

Shunar had just beaten two Frenchmen and was looking for more trouble when Carson told him to be quiet or he "would rip his guts." Shunar grabbed his rifle and mounted his horse. Carson seized the first weapon he could find, a pistol, galloped up to Shunar, and demanded if he was the one Shunar intended to shoot. As Carson continued in his autobiography:

> Our horses were touching. He said no, drawing his gun at the same time so he could have a shot at me. I was prepared and allowed him to draw his gun. We both fired at the same time, and all present said that but one report was heard. I shot him through the arm and his ball passed my head, cutting my hair and the powder burning my eye, the muzzle of his gun being near my head when he fired. During the remainder of our stay in camp we had no more bother with this French bully.

Reports conflicted for the next hundred years over whether Carson had killed Shunar. A decade after the fight, a Mrs. Benton remarked to Carson that he must have been in many fights. Carson said he had only been in one fight of his own, pushed his shirt collar aside, and showed the scar left by Shunar's bullet.

The panic of 1837 brought a sudden end to high prices for furs. The Indians couldn't understand American business and expected to receive as much for their furs as they always had, while the market abroad declined. The high beaver hat gave way to cheaper nutria fur, made from a rat found in Brazil, Argentina, and most of the fresh waters of South America. The French introduced silk hats and the English liked derbies made of wool. In short, the beaver trade was finished.

In 1843 Bridger and Louis Vasquez built Fort Bridger on Black's Fork of the Green River. There could have been no greater symbol that the fur trading days had ended: a stop for the convenience of emigrants set in the heart of the old fur country by a legendary mountain man. Captain Fremont reported in 1843 that the trappers had "almost entirely disappeared." James Clyman reported from Bridger's Fort the following year that there were fewer than thirty beaver hunters in the mountains. Wyoming's last great mountain man was Jim Baker, who trapped with Bridger, fought with

Jim Baker. (*Wyoming State Archives, Museums and Historical Dept.*)

grizzlies and Indians, and was adopted by the Shoshones. Baker built a log home on the Colorado-Wyoming border between Dixon and Savery, not far from where he fought the Cheyenne and Sioux in the battle that cost Fraeb his life. He died in 1898. In 1917 his two-story cabin was moved to Frontier Park in Cheyenne as a monument, but was moved back to Savery, Wyoming, in 1977.

The day of the fur trade may have passed, but its remarkable effects remained. Internationally, for centuries, the fur trade affected the schemes for power, wealth, and territorial influence in England, France, and Spain, and thus helped shape the New World. By the time attention reached Wyoming and the Rockies, the mountain men played critical roles in forging the final geographical boundaries in the West and Far West.

There were only about 1,000 mountain men, but during their short reign they explored the major mountains and valleys, rivers and streams of the region. Their knowledge led to the mapping of the West, and their intimate familiarity with the country enabled them to lead the wagon trains through it in later decades.

Throughout the United States, the noble beaver is remembered in countless places called Beaver Bay, Beaver River, Beaver Island, Beaver Creek, Beaver Falls, Beaverton, and Beaverdale. In Wyoming, there are Sublette County, Campbell County, Jackson Hole, Ashley National Forest, the Hoback Canyon and River, Fontenelle Reservoir, Colter Bay, Fort Laramie, Fort Bridger, the Sweetwater River, Independence Rock, and Devil's Gate—just a few of the places whose names have come down to us from the mountain men and their times.

Perhaps most of all, the mountain men represent to us a life full of romance and the pursuit of adventure, underlain by a strong sense of independence. In a technological, complex world they make us pause, for but a moment, not to long for fighting grizzlies, wild rivers, and starvation, but to contemplate all that we have gained, and with it, a sense of what we have lost.

THE SITES TODAY

The state of Wyoming does an excellent job of pointing out to travelers where historic events occurred, and many of these sites pertain to the mountain man era. In addition to the numerous sites along the highways, there is a number of places which dramatically recall the mountain man era. Some remain totally unchanged; others have been eroded by time or aided by reconstruction. Anyone interested in following some of the steps taken by these men will want to visit the following sites.

Fort Laramie

Built by William Sublette and Robert Campbell in 1833 as a strategic spot for trading furs, what became Fort Laramie was originally called Fort William, after William Sublette. Sublette and Campbell sold out to Jim Bridger, Thomas Fitzpatrick, and Milton Sublette in 1835, who sold the fort to the American Fur Company the following year.

The fort was visited by Rev. Samuel Parker and Dr. Marcus Whitman, early missionaries to Oregon, in 1835, and again in 1836 by Whitman and Mrs. Whitman with Rev. and Mrs. Henry H. Spaulding. Mrs. Whitman and Mrs. Spaulding were the first white women to travel the Oregon Trail.

In 1841 the American Fur Company replaced the deteriorating log stockade with an adobe-walled post and renamed it Fort John, probably after stockholder John Sarpy. But like its predecessor, Fort William, Fort John was popularly known as Fort Laramie, since it was located in the heart of the Laramie River country.

With the decline of the fur trade and the arrival of more emigrants on the Oregon Trail, Fort Laramie took on importance as a strategic supply post. Fremont recommended that the fort become a military post while visiting the area in 1849. After playing host to a party under Dr. Whitman in 1843 and the emigrating Mormons in 1947, the fort was

Fort Laramie. (From *Stansbury's Expedition to the Great Salt Lake*)

Fort William, 1837, by Alfred Jacob Miller. (*Fort Laramie National Historic Site, National Park Service*)

The remains of the non-commissioned officers' quarters at Fort Laramie stand like weathered Greek columns, reminders of a long lost day. (*Richard L. Fetter*)

purchased by the federal government in 1849. After the discovery of gold in California in that year, thousands of travelers stopped annually at the fort for rest, repairs, and supplies.

By the 1870s and 1880s Fort Laramie had become the most significant military post on the northern plains, serving as a Pony Express and Overland Stage station, a base for campaigns against the Indians and important treaties with them, and finally as a supply center and source of protection for the ranchers and homesteaders of the 1870s.

The fort was abandoned in 1890 and fell into neglect and decay until 1937, when Wyoming donated the 214 acres of the former military post to the federal government for the creation of the Fort Laramie National Historic Site in 1938.

Today this site, as much as any place you can visit, offers a sense of the isolation and loneliness of the Western army officer or traveler in the nineteenth century. In the center of the fort is the large parade ground, surrounded by the officers' quarters, sutler's store, "Old Bedlam" (Wyoming's oldest standing military structure), the captain's quarters, and remains of the new and old guardhouses. There is no fence around the fort. In the distance are Laramie Peak, the old cemetery, and traces of the Oregon Trail.

The site is open all year except Christmas and New Year's Day and is administered by the National Park Service. From mid-June to Labor Day, the hours are 7-7; the rest of the year 8-4:30. Groups wishing guided tours are requested to make arrangements in advance with the superintendent.

Register Cliffs

Located 13 miles west of Fort Laramie at Guernsey, Register Cliffs is one of three places in Wyoming where emigrants camped along the Oregon Trail and left their names carved in the soft chalky cliffs. This is one of the best sites in terms of number and legibility of the carvings, many of which date from the late 1840s and early 1850s.

Oregon Trail Ruts National Monument

Located south of Guernsey, not far from Register Cliffs, this national monument marks the place where thousands of wagons rolled over the Oregon Trail and wore down the soft rock. The site will leave a lasting impression upon anyone who finds a sense of history in being precisely where history was made, even touching it. Perhaps someday the ruts will be fenced off to prevent deterioration, but this has not yet happened. The ruts are deeply embedded in the rock, oblivious to blowing sands, prairie winds, and modern visitors who can readily imagine the long caravans, clanking wheels, and tired but unflagging hopes of our ancestors bound for Oregon.

Independence Rock

In April 1830, William Sublette set out for the Wind River rendezvous with a caravan of goods from St. Louis, deter-

Independence Rock, once "the Register of the Desert."
(*Richard L. Fetter*)

mined to see if wagons could make it up the Platte and over South Pass.

On July 4 the caravan stopped on the Sweetwater River at the isolated igneous rock formation which today is called Independence Rock, possibly named by Sublette at that time. The rock became a well-known landmark along the Oregon Trail. Father De Smet called it "The Great Register of the Desert," estimating that some 40,000 names were painted, carved, or written on its surface.

The great rock lies along an ancient animal trail which was followed by Indians and then the mountain men and subsequent travelers along the Oregon Trail. Today it lies conspicuously off State Highway 220, 50 miles west of Casper. Access to the rock is easy and some of the names may still be seen, but lichen and time have slowly covered the majority of them.

South Pass, still bleak and almost forgotten. The discovery of its gentle inclines led to the Oregon Trail and the opening of the Northwest. (*Richard L. Fetter*)

Devil's Gate

Located five miles west of Independence Rock, this was another famous landmark for both the mountain man and Oregon Trail traveler. A deep gorge cut through the Rattlesnake Mountains by the Sweetwater River, Devil's Gate is a dramatic site that today may be visited by a series of walking paths originating just off the main highway.

South Pass and South Pass City

Today's traveler in the Rockies will probably be quite familiar with the high passes of the Rocky Mountains by the time he reaches South Pass and South Pass City. Whether we're familiar with Colorado, Idaho, Montana, or Wyoming routes, we can easily imagine the difficulty a laden horse, not to mention a wagon, had making its way through the endless rocks and precarious cliffs of the Rocky Mountain chain.

One gazes in wonder, therefore, at the open expanse of South Pass and marvels at the ease with which the continental divide can be crossed here, much as it was a century and a half ago.

Coming from the east, the route, now Highway 28, passes the striking red cliffs of a canyon, twists and turns past the iron mine near Atlantic City, passes the turnoff for South Pass City, and levels off into a broad, undulating plateau marked by a few cattle and horses, some resting pronghorns, scrub pine, and the distant peaks of Shoshone and Bridger-Teton National Forests. Rising, then dipping only to rise again, the highway climbs steadily but at times imperceptibly until it reaches the summit, which is marked only by an elevation marker at 7,550 feet. It is not surprising that Fremont said he hardly knew when the summit had been reached. Without the marker, nor would we.

A few miles beyond, a roadside marker shows the "parting of the ways," the fork in the old trail. Right led to Oregon, left went to Utah and California. Somewhere in these barren wastes, Stuart led the returning Astorians in 1812. The Ashley-Henry party crossed westbound in 1824, and by the peak emigration year of 1852, an estimated 40,000 people had crossed South Pass.

In 1842 a Georgian traveling with the American Fur Company discovered gold in the South Pass City area. He was killed on his way back east to get backing for a mining venture, and no more prospecting took place until 1855. It may be logical to suppose that South Pass City grew to meet the needs of the emigrants crossing the Oregon Trail, but the truth is that it developed as a mining town when gold was discovered in 1867. By then, emigrant travel on the Oregon Trail had greatly subsided.

Mark Twain passed through in the early 1860s and described in *Roughing It* how South Pass City was four log cabins, one of which was unfinished, and ten citizens. His party was met by the hotel-keeper, postmaster, blacksmith, mayor, constable, city marshal, principal citizen, and property holder, "and we gave him good day."

South Pass City holds the distinction of being the birthplace of women's suffrage in America. Prompted by the initiative of Esther Hobart Morris and others, W. H. Bright of South Pass City introduced a bill in the Wyoming legislature to give women the right to vote. The bill passed and became law in 1869. South Pass City has burned down three times. The buildings that exist there today are original to different periods. None dates back to 1869. Most are from the late 1890s to 1920.

Although often referred to as a ghost town, South Pass City has not died. A small handful of state site workers and one private citizen continue to live there year-round, braving what can sometimes be a very long winter. The site is administered jointly by the Wyoming State Archives Museum, and History Department and the Wyoming Recreation Commission.

South Pass City. (*Richard L. Fetter*)

Cody

Anyone interested in the mountain man era and the times it ushered in will want to visit the Buffalo Bill Historical Center at Cody, featuring the Plains Indian Museum. Remington collection of firearms, and Whitney Gallery of Western Art. The art collection includes works by Alfred Jacob Miller, whose paintings of the mountain man era are among the few visual records we have of that time.

A few miles west of Cody is a roadside marker pointing out Colter's Hell. Although there are some references to Colter's Hell being the geysers at Yellowstone, the name actually refers to the semi-active geyser basin near U.S. Highways 14, 16, and 20, two miles west of town.

Also of interest is the Trail Town Museum outside Cody on the road to Yellowstone, just before the Colter's Hell marker. The small museum consists of a collection of old buildings, artifacts, and a monument to the mountain man placed by the Mountain Men of America. Three mountain men of a slightly later era are buried there, including "Liver-eatin" Johnson, whose story was told in the movie *Jeremiah Johnson* a few years ago.

Grand Teton National Park Headquarters, Moose

The Visitor's Center contains an excellent display of the mountain man period, complete with relics, drawings, photographs, and displays. The story of the mountain men is told simply and interestingly, and the displays include the mysterious Colter Stone, either a hoax or the proof that John Colter wintered in Pierre's Hole on his famous 1807 trip.

Names Hill

Names Hill is the third and westernmost of the three places in Wyoming where Oregon Trail travelers rested and carved their names in the neighboring rock cliffs. It is conveniently located just off Highway 189, a few miles south

Jim Bridger's name carved at Names Hill. (*Richard L. Fetter*)

of La Barge. The site is highlighted by the carved name of "James Bridger, Trapper 1844," which is curious in light of the fact that the famous scout was supposed to be illiterate. The authenticity of the carving has been questioned. The belief is that either Bridger could write his name, or someone did it for him at the time he was there.

Fort Bridger

If Fort Laramie leaves an impression of isolation and loneliness out on the western plains, recalling images of soldiers marching around the great parade ground or disappearing over the hill to save the settlers, Fort Bridger creates a sense of how such forts brought civilization to the frontier. Located between Green River and Evanston in the southwestern corner of Wyoming, Fort Bridger is smaller than Fort Laramie and located in the small town of Fort Bridger, which would account for the sense of relative coziness. But in addition there is a certain warmth in the stone and log houses themselves. Especially in the commanding officer's quarters, with its white picket fence and small wooded area in front, there is a feeling of civilization and

Fort Bridger. (From *Stansbury's Expedition to the Great Salt Lake*)

order as well as refuge. The general change in terrain was observed by Horace Greeley in 1859, who referred to Fort Bridger as "the terminus in this direction of the Great American Desert."

When Jim Bridger and Louis Vasquez completed their little trading post here in 1843, it consisted of a few crude log buildings and nothing more. The fort served as supply post to local Indians and passing emigrants, some of the first of which were Mormons fleeing from persecution back east. In 1855 when Bridger was reportedly away from the post, Vasquez sold the post to the Mormons, but they burned and abandoned it in 1857 when the army, led by Colonel Johnston and guided by Bridger, was dispatched to the area.

In 1858 the army built a permanent fort here, and Colonel Johnston named it in honor of Bridger. Fort Bridger remained an active military post until 1890, when many of the buildings were sold at a public auction. Some of these are still in use as homes. In its day, the fort served as a Pony Express stop and an Overland Stage station. It also was the home of W. A. Carter, post sutler, who owned one of Wyoming's largest livestock operations. Among Carter's many contributions to the area was the creation of the first school in Wyoming. The building is one of several that can be seen at the fort. Others include the sutler's store, officers' quarters, and museum. In addition the visitor can see the tracks of wagon trains, now overgrown with grass, where they passed through en route to California, Utah, and Oregon.

Every Labor Day weekend Fort Bridger recreates the biggest rendezvous west of the Mississippi, a great three-day affair that annually attracts up to 15,000 people, including 400-500 "buckskinners" who come to trade, barter, and celebrate the long gone but still very much alive mountain man era.

Fort Bridger is open daily April 1-October 15; weekends only October 16-March 31. Admission is free. For special tours call (307) 782-3842. The site is administered jointly by the Wyoming State Archives, Museum and History Department and the Wyoming Recreation Commission.

The mountain man's gear and way of life are kept alive today at places like Fort Bridger, Dubois, Henry's Fork, and Pinedale, where people gather annually from all over the country to celebrate the rendezvous. This collection belongs to Ron Schrotter, "Brigade Booshway," or president, of the Wyoming Chapter of the Rocky Mountain Mountain Men Association. The 1870 Green River knife is an original, found in a forgotten corner of the Hudson Bay Co. headquarters in London a few years ago.
(Richard L. Fetter)

NOTES

Page

5 (Lewis requirements) Letter, Meriwether Lewis to William Clark, June 19, 1803, quoted in *Original Journals*, VII, 227, cited in Hafen, *Fur Trade*, VIII, 74.

8 (Bridger) E.R. Schauffler (*Kansas City Times*, January 10, 1940), cited in Hafen, *Fur Trade*, VI, 104.

10 (Colter) Thomas James, *Three Years Among the Indians and Mexicans*, ed. by W. B. Douglas (St. Louis, 1916), 65-66, cited in Hafen, *Fur Trade*, VIII, 84.

15 (Bridger on Laramie) Grace R. Hebard and E.A. Brininstool, *The Bozeman Trail*, 233.

22 (4th of July) Hafen, *Fur Trade*, III, 257.

22 (grog and trade) Dale Morgan and Eleanor Harris, *The Rocky Mountain Journals of William Marshall Anderson* (San Marino, the Huntington Library, 1867), 27, cited in Gowans, *Rocky Mountain Rendezvous*, 141.

22 (running, jumping) Delmont R. Oswald, ed., *The Life and Adventures of James P. Beckwourth as Told to Thomas D. Bonner* (Lincoln, University of Nebraska Press, 1972), 107, cited in Gowans, *Rocky Mountain Rendezvous*, 22.

24 (Bridger tale) Anson Mills, *My Story* (Washington, D.C. 1918), 107, 109, cited in Hafen, *Fur Trade*, VI, 100.

26 (closest calculation) T.D. Bonner, *The Life and Adventures of James P. Beckwourth*, (New York, 1856), 123-24, cited in Hafen, *Fur Trade*, VI, 44.

28 (grissly Baare) "James Clyman, His Diaries and Reminiscences," ed. by Charles L. Camp, *California Historical Society Quarterly* (1925), Vol. IV, 122-23, cited in Robert Glass Cleland, *This Reckless Breed of Men*, 59.

30 (bustle in camp) Maurice Sullivan, *The Travels of Jedediah Smith* (Santa Ana, California, 1934), 2, cited in Cleland, *This Reckless Breed of Men*, 85.

34 (Newell to Meek) Frances Fuller Victor, *River of the West*, (Brooks-Sterling Company, Oakland 1974), 264-

65, cited in Gowans, *Rocky Mountain Rendezvous*, 258.
38 (Astor on beaver) H.M. Chittenden, *The American Fur Trade*, I, 365.
40 (Shunar fight) Kit Carson, *Autobiography*, 42-44.
42 (Fremont on mountain men) P.C. Phillips, *The Fur Trade*, II, 526.

BIBLIOGRAPHY

Bonner, T. D. *The Life and Adventures of James P. Beckwourth.* New York: Chas. D. Leland, 1856.

Berry, Don. *A Majority of Scoundrels.* New York: Harper & Brothers, 1961.

Carson, Kit. *Autobiography.* Chicago: Lakeside Press, 1935.

Camp, Charles L. *James Clyman, Frontiersman.* Portland, Ore.: Champoeg Press, 1960.

——————. "James Clyman, His Diaries and Reminiscences." *California Historical Society Quarterly* (1925), Vol. IV, No. 2.

Chittenden, Hiram M. *The American Fur Trade of the Far West.* New York: Press of the Pioneers, 1935.

Cleland, Robert G. *This Reckless Breed of Men: Trappers and Fur Traders of the Southwest.* New York: Alfred A. Knopf, 1950.

Coutant, C. G. *History of Wyoming.* Volume One. Laramie: Chaplin, Spafford, & Mathison, 1899.

Dale Harrison C. *The Ashley-Smith Explorations, 1822-1829.* Cleveland: Arthur H. Clark, 1918.

——————. *Fort Bridger State Historical Site.* Museum Division, Wyoming State Archives Museum and Historical Department and the Wyoming Recreation Commission (undated pamphlet).

Gowans, Fred R. *Rocky Mountain Rendezvous: A History of the Fur Trade Rendezvous, 1825-1840.* Provo, Utah: Brigham Young University Press, 1975.

Hafen, LeRoy R. *The Mountain Men and the Fur Trade of the Far West.* Ten Volumes. Glendale, Calif.: Arthur H. Clark Co., 1964-1972.

Hebard, Grace R. and E. A. Brininstool. *The Bozeman Trail.* Two volumes. Cleveland: Arthur H. Clark Co., 1922.

Hieb, David L. *Fort Laramie National Historic Site.* National Park Service Historical Handbook Series No. 20. Washington, D.C., 1954.

Irving, Washington. *Astoria.* Philadelphia: Carey, Lea & Blanchard, 1836.

James, Thomas. *Three Years Among the Indians and Mexicans*, Ed. by W. B. Douglas. St. Louis: Missouri Historical Society, 1916.

Lawrence, Paul. *John Colter, Journey of Discovery*, Jackson, Wyo: Unita Pioneer Press, 1978.

Mattes, Merrill J. *Colter's Hell & Jackson Hole.* Yellowstone Library and Museum Association and Grand Teton Natural History Association, 1962.

Mills, Anson. *My Story*, Washington, D.C., 1918.

Morgan, Dale L. *Jedediah Smith and the Opening of the West.* Lincoln: University of Nebraska Press, 1964.

_____________. *The West of William H. Ashley, 1822-1838.* Denver: The Old West Publishing Company, 1964.

Morgan, Dale L. and Eleanor Harris. *The Rocky Mountain Journals of William Marshall Anderson.* San Marino, Calif.: The Huntington Library, 1967.

Phillips, P. C. *The Fur Trade.* Vol. II. Norman: University of Oklahoma Press, 1961.

Russell, Osborne. *Journal of a Trapper.* Ed. by Aubrey L. Haines. Lincoln: University of Nebraska Press, 1965.

Schauffler, E. R. *Kansas City Times.* January 10, 1940.

Sullivan, Maurice, *The Travels of Jedediah Smith.* Santa Ana, Calif.: Fine Arts Press, 1934.

Thwaites, Reuben Gold, ed. *Original Journals of the Lewis and Clark Expedition.* New York: Arno, 1904, Vol. VII.

Twain, Mark. *Roughing It.* New York: Harper & Brothers, 1913.

Victor, Frances Fuller. *River of the West.* Oakland: Brooks-Sterling Company, 1974.

Acknowledgements

While following the trail of the old mountain men across Wyoming, I was fortunate enough to meet several people who kindly contributed their time and expertise and lent an appreciated hand. In particular, I wish to thank Ralph Stock, Curator of Interpretative Services, and Paula West, Supervisor of Photographic Collections, Wyoming State Museum, Cheyenne; Mike Kelly, Librarian and Archivist, Buffalo Bill Historical Center, Cody; Michael Livingston, Supervisory Historian, Fort Laramie National Historic Site, Fort Laramie; Tom Lindmier, Curator, Fort Bridger State Museum, Fort Bridger; and Ron Schrotter, President, Wyoming Chapter, Rocky Mountain Mountain Men Association.